CROSSINGS

Janneth Mornan-Green

ABENG
PRESS

Mornan-Green, Janneth
Crossings

ISBN 978-0-9867253-4-0

1. Anthology. 2. Jamaica - Poetry. 3. Caribbean - Poetry
Book design by Beresford Nicholson, Abeng Press
Cover design by Louis Matalon

Published in Canada by
Abeng Press

www.AbengPress.com

To:

Freddy who believed and Kathryn who listened with patience and supported my effort.

The members of the Andrews Memorial SDA Church Poetry Society who motivated and provided an outlet.

My lifelong friend Sydney Roberts whose faith never wavered; my brother Vincent Mornan and my niece Joan Dougherty who not only read but critiqued and encouraged.

Former student, friend and teacher Craig Dixon who inspires and reminds me that "we don't have forever to dream".

Special thanks to award winning writer and friend Jean Goulbourne who took the time to assess and suggest ways to improve the poems selected for this publication.

Dedicated to the memory of my father Vincent; mother Gertrude; brothers Fitzroy and Ali and sister Norma.

These poems first appeared in Bookends in Jamaica's Sunday Observer: *Sub-titles, Close-up, Falling into Eye, Before, Closure, Tell Me, Zombie, Snapshot, Morning Coffee, Webmaster, Sunday Stupor.*

"But to do good and to communicate forget not:
for with such sacrifices God is well pleased."
Hebrews 13:16.

CONTENTS

III

I

The nerve of life tingles more acutely
with each encounter.

Sub-titles

On some obscure mornings
when I rifle through my thoughts
searching for *HEADLINES*
I am confronted by *sub-titles*

Like today, watching
Pelicans Dive in Port Royal Bay
looking for a poem at the end
of a fisherman's rod
or epiphany in sea salt.

Perhaps there's a story in the
waves; in winged hunters who
thwart the sea wind
and barnacles multiplying,
their sum etched on the sea wall.

Janneth Mornan-Green

Art

Brush weeps blood
red strokes,
vermilion, blue
paint
precise breaths on canvas
splashing life into dead form
a man, a woman
a pansy, a daisy
animals, peasants,
princes imprisoned in colour,
shades,
a kaleidoscope of moments.
At the end of brush strokes
Mona Lisa, Sunflowers, Irises
Sistine Chapel
sealing blood, sweat, tears
into art.

Christmas Past

That evening Death came
to our house without invitation
it slipped in the front door
when no-one was looking
and hid under my grandmother's bed.

Unknowing, she'd asked for cheese
forgetting that it gave her diarrhea
and the myth that says if you suddenly
ate what you had stopped eating,
you could end up dead.

It was two days past Christmas
the house still wore the season,
its red, white and tinsel
waiting to be gone like the visitors
who just days before had been anxious to arrive.

So Death switched the colours,
painted it winter, as dusk shrouded
itself in the usual ritual,
kerosene lamplight, camphor balls and bay rum
the usual lament, "I wish you children would stop your noise.
Gertrude, you know if George will come tonight?"

That night as the house slept
in its shiny Christmas dress
Death took my grandfather's place.
He began at her toes, feathering cold kisses along her thighs
stroking her belly, nibbling her throat, closing her eyes.

A sharp note rolled down my father's cheek
and pooled amid his violin strings
my mother's Singer sewing machine
knew no rest until she had pedalled miles
tucking and pleating, interring selvedge and trim
gathering up the threads of all our lives.

Janneth Mornan-Green

Rosie

(for George, my grandfather)

By the time he came
she was sheeted in white
reposed in the centre
of the single bed
kerosene lamp
shadowing the mood
of a cold December evening.

The hum of mourners
like breeze whiffling through
bamboo leaves drew him
"Nearer my God to Thee"
as he entered the room
reluctantly heeding
the beckon of her still form.

He stripped, as familiar lovers do
after time has transformed passion
into a meticulous ritual
and with deliberateness
prostrated himself upon the stiff,
lifeless form whispering
"Rosie".

Country Life

In those days when Enterprise's horn
would woo passengers
Ben Lowe wooed the village girls,
promised Kingston -
lights bright and far and mysterious
no water-boots or water pails

his un-zippered offers
opened Pandora's box wide.

Later, many wished they had left
his silver tongued lures behind.

Janneth Mornan-Green

For Gertrude
(My mother who died in 1999)

The news came like a tropical downpour; sudden.
She had not eaten in days and I wondered how she felt,
how she silenced the questions raised by a belly that seemed
always to have been full - with children, ideas, expectations, disappointment
how she eased the panic trapped by a lifeless tongue
or tamed the babble as her mind disgorged each memory
like bats exiting a house at twilight.

Stroke! Stroke!
The relentless refrain pitched in sharps and flats
floated on the staves of evening,
each note the hand of a determined clock, striking closer to midnight.

Time raced to its appointment,
a hierophant, impatient to reveal an unfathomable truth
as the universe unburdened itself beside her bed,
her story a shadowy scrawl, composed in the creases of wrinkled sheets
and on curtains fluttering hopelessly against the wall.
Outside, Sunday rode in on silent wings
paused beneath the traceries; contemplative, still
to witness the dissolution, the de-center-ing of things.

A Moment of Silence

Like impatient waves
imprisoned in a shell,
racing tide caught by the shoreline

or noisy speeches
locked behind pursed lips
words tripping
over themselves
to escape,

a moment of silence comes
pulling opaque curtains over solemn faces
shuttering emotions
yearning to flash free
of regret.

Janneth Mornan-Green

"MAD"

Cocooned;
layered in skirts, blouses,
multi-coloured stockings
armoured against the world,
she patrols the churchyard
a perplexed pleat
sits long on her brow
life's complexities secure within its fold

she sings comfort songs
pure, clear testimony
perhaps of secret longing

something inside awaits opportunity
to be free.

Rite of Passage

You would marvel at the extent to which some people have to
be their own security guards, running surveillance for their daughters
even before they reach puberty; for tenements are not tolerant of virgins
and Maas Charlie who waits at his door each Sunday morning rubbing the
spaces between his toes, bringing his fingers to his nose and returning
them to whatever pleasure awaits his olfactory between the cracks,
is hoping for opportunity to open a window so he can invade like a
European explorer. And don't bother to believe that when Miss Joyce left
Mavis locked up in the room that Sunday morning she had a chance.
The fact that she had carried Mavis around like a prize-handbag for twelve
years didn't stop Maas Charlie from forcing the window open wide, wide
and the loud creaking and shrieking didn't bring the neighbours running
because after years of learning how to be invisible in a tenement,
everybody is an expert in "see and blind, hear and deaf;" and
further, the forcing of a window has long been recognized in those parts
as a virgin's rite of passage.

Janneth Mornan-Green

the pedal pusher

dead eyes
fixed to an unseen target
the pedal pusher
cycles
on the wrong side of the road
blank pupils
eloquent
of his 'paradise lost'

anguish
propels motion
down the up side
of Constant Spring
jaws locked,
as if in concentration
hope ebbing with each revolution

i saw him
and i thought
what if?
what if he could see
the wheels turn like me?
would the vacant mask
lose its indifference
and embrace the turbulence
of life?

Dragonflies...

... crowding Cherry Drive
in an evening dance
swarm happily back and forth
to and fro oblivious
of the sadness of
separation

their moves, a seamless choreography
floating on the fading beams
eyes blind to grief,
to a mind in chaos like a fix-less addict
lost in an adrenaline rush.

On the edge
of twilight, a frantic soul
searches for purpose in metamorphosis,
in graceful wings soaring in the ritual
of a death-dance

for meaning in
happy dragonflies
 crystal wings
filtering late evening rays,
dancing.

Janneth Mornan-Green

Tea Leaves

If a clairvoyant read his palm
the interest would not be his lifeline
but time's residue lodged
beneath broken finger nails,
narratives in skin
ripped like exhausted almanac leaves,
scars defying the certainty
of tea leaf patterns.

If a clairvoyant looked
the mystery of the supernatural would flee
leaving life behind.

Death Reveals Secrets

There is exhilaration in grief;
a nervous anticipation in the ritual
of lamentation, of earth and ash mingling
with the smell of roses,
of the spectacle of interment
blurred by tears.

Like a hot air balloon
that has sailed too long among the clouds
he drifted to rest amid the flowers of an eternal meadow.

He sleeps but there is no rapid eye movement to
gauge the depth of his dreams
or the intensity of his ride on the headless mare
galloping to an unknown destiny.

He had seen many places, heard many stories
measured his emotions on the frets of his guitar
stringing the melody of his village and island
over continents, inspired by the rhythm of nostalgia.

Now, eulogized in a list of ordinary events
no-one recounts the excitement of his many lovers
no notes proclaim the music he made
no prose his thoughts
no concealed diaries his disappointments

only his children know the women he loved
only he knew why he had left.

When death comes, secrets die;
death reveals secrets.

Janneth Mornan-Green

Flowers

He sent me plastic roses
"For the wife," he'd said

certain he wouldn't see the day
when I'd be adorned in white
real flowers clutched tightly,
my brother's arm guiding my uncertain gait
as I stepped … stepped …
and mentally fussed with my dress, my shoes.

I didn't remember him then
not until the wedding feast
when someone said
"Witter wished he could be here."

As we chased mirth with wine
somewhere there was weeping
and I remembered that only days before
his soul had gone to sleep.

Stitches

He had promised a sewing machine.
Then, she had been the village beauty
and he had said the only thing sweeter than her
were the golden pegs of the jackfruit
just at the peak of fullness.

She didn't like jackfruit
too sticky, too sweet
but she dreamed of stitching a patchwork of opportunity
and she didn't have a clue about the pitfalls of "pressa foot."
Not yet.

The machine could stitch drapes
and the bed, like the table, would have a cover
to hide the roughness under
to stop the moon from uncovering the secret that
not even her own mother could detect;
the nightly desire to moult
every time he touched her.

In fact she had only allowed him to touch her
because he seemed so sure about the machine
and she was so certain that she could endure anything
for a Singer with spools and a bobbin
as the sound it made kept replaying itself in her head;
she'd heard it the seven times she went to "lying in"
and every night after, as the years
started unraveling one, one.
She heard it every time Fallda the extractor
entered the district and her mouth with his pliers;
the melody rocked her to sleep, when her man stopped
coming, except to visit the children.

And the rhythm of the stitching has woven
such a strong tapestry of sound through the years
that forty anniversaries later she can still hear
the whirring as she mimics the
looping of the thread with her fingers and
imagines a camel squeezing his hump through the needle's eye
while she begs Massa God to grant her one wish.

Janneth Mornan-Green

Close-up

I tore the picture in two
the one with me and you seated
by the washtub
covered in suds and smiles.

It seemed the right thing to do
to erase the myth,
the frozen image of the pose;
such a negative to those who knew

how quickly time rearranged
the view, the mask coming askew
to expose the fable in the frame
and replace the bliss

with the bare, unadorned portrait
of just us two.

For C.D.

You told me your story of deprivation
days spent trawling the long Pell River grass,
rustling words
rivaling life's cacophony
your pen defying the ills
that threatened to ambush your dreams

images emerged
as melancholia multiplied;
visions clutched the olive branch of hope
recasting algid concrete
and the stickiness of sugar cane
into art

until here you are
saved by
a poem
plucking at the chords of your imagination.

Janneth Mornan-Green

Parakeet Hill at Easter

The narrative of the house is forever altered
by your short story
told in inquiring footsteps, halting to examine
my world - a tale of exclusivity
and the curiosity of stifling smoke from burning peat
ignited by spontaneous combustion.

Across the plains and up the hillside
the withered grass has forgotten spring
the brown river bends to the sea
whispering your thoughts to the birds perched
upon the lonely bridge

the chattering parakeets will not disclose your secrets
neither will the leaves repeat your private conversations,
your dreams are safe with the fishes that swim the shallows
at Crab Thatch Bay, ferrying your fears to the anonymity of the ocean.

In this place your heart is a bird's wing
beating back the silence of the future,
silencing the terror of possibilities.

II

Perhaps life is best expressed in sighs
and its mystery sustained when we wonder why.

Falling into Eye

Your look
penetrated
the lid of my desires,
dilating everything.

Janneth Mornan-Green

Jugando Con Fuego

In a once quiet crevasse of my mind
an inferno rages
cadmium yellow flames
impatiently reaching up with forked tongue
to lick the flap of memory

The heat levitates like haze
until every corner burns
and thought is incinerated
in the consuming blaze

The smoke of my emotions
rises; a burnt offering.
But on this altar of sacrifice
there is no benediction.

Jugando con fuego
Jugando con fuego

You're playing with fire!

The Windflower's song

Were it not for a stranger's hand
you would not have stumbled across my path that day
shy, uncertain, buttoned in your self containment
escorted by the echo of a restless odyssey

Were it not for duty
I would not have stood, adorned in arrogance
even as my Babel was being razed
by confounding metaphors

Were it not for your pen
I'd not have learnt the syntax of your sighs
or the eloquence of a silence
rooted in your mythology.

In the existing void your melody remains
like the song the windflower sings
petals opening to the breeze
that takes its breath away

In your absence is your presence
stronger than Gibraltar
more sure than the knowledge
that dawn brings day.

Janneth Mornan-Green

Contained

The mountains lie rigid;
fixed, like surveyors' instruments
trained upon an invisible line.

Deep in the valley, silence is
sentinel. Thoughts bottled.
Contained. Bound.

Tension vibrates…
its quiver caught by a chorus of fiddling crickets
twanging the strings of twilight;
dropping its cadence, as if from a distance
into the dusky stillness.

Fog fondles the treetops
stroking the canopy,
a tight viridian canvas
stretched upon the hillside.

The tired evening sighs
as the mountains squat,
line drawn, ears cocked
in mute watchfulness.

Prosaic words conceal the damp intimacy of rain,
of beached waves frothing on the sand
trailing frilly seaweed …
and the memory of wine

the mountains increase their scrutiny.

Weary joggers relay their narrative
in deliberate strides and sweat,
lapping the track in ones and twos
exiting to enter to exit

mutual silence erects
a citadel; thoughts
imprisoned in the gaze of mountains,
alien emotions
too timid to transform them into words.

ii

On some distant rain-hazed evening
I too shall recall the bottled silence of a May twilight
the gentle brush of uneasy fingers,
the confused quest of an outstretched hand

I too shall wander deserted corridors
entering and exiting concealed rooms
looking occasionally through the telescope of time
like a surveyor, his instruments fixed,
trained upon an invisible line.

Janneth Mornan-Green

Caveat Emptor (Fantasy)

I was young again.
You halted
my unwilling feast at
the teats of time,
Your smile
a prop for my uncertainty

My light
hot
flashed quicksilver
caught
in your penetrating heat.

Spring arrived
in the fecund pages of your opus

ii

Yet
you came stealthily
your enchanted pen
corseting life's bulges
expressions
a banquet for desiccated emotions

Your metaphors
demolished *caveat emptor*

How could time compete with your vocabulary?

Spring arrived
and I embraced
the paradox
of abstruse emotions
lost in the rhythm of a poem.

Of Alien Towers

The night walks swiftly.
At 20 MPH I am a nuisance
the crawl, an anomaly.
My heart is not in sync;
it races.

The diamond lights of the city spread
a galaxy at the feet of winding streets.
The radio pleads "Lord, I want to be a witness"
I hope for the contrary -

against the curtain of the night
no applause, no encore
no signs or well lit exit door
only the bricks of alien towers.

"*Let me tell you the story of how I got to be young*"
That's the crux.
The antique syllables of my story creak,
the oil has leaked from their hinges.

There is pathos in the things unsaid
like mute flowers left to guard the dead.

Janneth Mornan-Green

Ring Road

Tonight, I'll take the journey
"Just one more time, please?"
                              Circling,
slowly winding time in circuitous loops
trying to detain it for an extended hour.
Not traversing the seamless golden circle
to dance on its perpetual treadmill
or slicing through the mystery of annulus
to gauge the revolutions of the clock
but peeling back the bark
to touch the softness of evening.

The night will be the cynic it always is

                    A ring, a ring o' roses
                    A pocket full o' posies
                    Tishoo, tishoo,
                    All fall down!

Regardless,
like a vespertine command, twilight will find us
caught in a loop
courting time;
circling.

When the Crickets Sing

That night, the crickets' song was an alarm
its gong reverberating on the humid air,
whistling like hurricane through
the splayed fingers of the breadfruit;
havoc!

Passion was an urgent mouth
the certainty of a glass blower's hands
the bloody arrows of ginger lilies
pointed, fixed

then plucked and strewn;
shifting sand in a sand dune,
the granules grinding
each against each
like crickets' wings
composing a call to flight.

Now, when the crickets
stridulate a nighttime serenade
I'll find you in its refrain
I'll hear your measured tone
urging san-it-y and in-te-grit-y
and your resolve in their relentless chorus of the night.

Janneth Mornan-Green

The Power of a Flower

Through the thickness of a brooding evening
seagulls hover, gleaming over luminous water;
sterile clouds shroud the sun
as it peers through the puffs to find its reflection.
In this strange hour
the birds fill the twilight's silence with their calling
the eerie half-light blackening the green hills in the distance.
Against these static scenes
your restlessness reflects a mood
skewed by your internal history;
it is out of step, caught in a modern quandary.

As our sand-caked feet
nudge the chunks of brittle coral
glimmering white along the beach,
dusk wraps up the day
luring grizzled men to their surveillance points
to interpret time's riddles
for they have tasted life's truths
the bitterness of its mystery no source of consolation.
Secure in the confines of their cabal
solutions seem clearer than a Supreme thought,
reality, no match for their fragile coalitions.

Your heart is a pulsating fist
outpacing the unremitting waves that pummel the coastline
for you crave engagement with the world, not isolation;
not the desire to fill your belly with the unfortunate legacies of old men.
The beauty of the seascape is swallowed in the vortex
of your dreams, a tangle of cross roads
inter-twined by insidious anxiety.
The uncertainty of hidden mysteries
coalesce in the navel of your ambitions
painting quivering patterns
on the edge of sunset

Locked, each in our thoughts
we retrace our steps
the antics of the evening people
vying for a moment to rivet fickle attention.
A lustrous flower arrests
your interest, and as with care
you fasten it to my hair
it seems enough;
in the thickness of twilight
your world is now calm
amid the cries of the gulls.

Janneth Mornan-Green

Silhouette

Today the sun sketched you,
a silhouette in charcoal
against the frame of evening.
You laughed as the greedy wind
swallowed your voice,
emitting echoes.

Later, I watched as
beguiled by the guipure foam,
you kissed the coral
lips of the sea

and saw it arch its back
and wave,
leaving you adrift.

A Different Kind of Leaving

And you said
'Control' is a good thing
to be desired, cultivated;
necessary to subdue emotion,
contain it.

And I said
control is a corset
fashioned from a designed experience.

So now we remain
buckled in strait-jackets of our own choosing
confined to a different kind of leaving.

Janneth Mornan-Green

The Witness

Looking through the aperture of my anxieties
I view again the tissued folds that hold
"Free Ixora";
its petals are now like bars
its skeleton leaving a deep imprint
as our feet did in the sand.

But like footprints in the sand that vanish
when the moon entices the errant tide
to take shore leave,
Ixora too has waned.
Soon it will disappear
as memory fades to black.

Cliché

To say you broke my heart
would be a cliché
and you know how I hate clichés.
After all, it's not as if my heart
fell off a shelf or you had an accident.
I gave it to you
and I guess, as with all gifts
you felt you had the right
to treasure it or trash it.
So you did.

Janneth Mornan-Green

Before

Before,
I had been as hopeful as Christmas Carols
that the poems I had packed for evening
would be as creaseless as your guarantee,
which seemed so unassailable at the time.
I had seen them hanging in your window
where the light transformed their lines
into the purest symmetry,
and convinced myself that they would fit
and fall gloriously to my feet.

Wrinkles are such sobering things.
They make you think that nothing creased
can ever be made smooth again.

Washday

And yet, any number of scenarios could have evolved
If I had read the words scribbled on the lines of your
face more accurately, I would have walked away;
left, holding my head where I'd always held it - fastened to
my shoulders, my wits anchored in experience and my pride
an envelope for my integrity

I could have ignored the ache every time your eyes shot arrows
or your lyrics made me forget that stars die, flowers fade and
darkness always follows light; and if I had chosen to remember
that life's road is full of blind corners and that this may have been one
I'd have hugged the curve, navigating cautiously

but I chose the deliberateness of risk, folding your promises like clean
laundry, placing them in neat piles; and now like a disillusioned housewife
on washday, I'm reminded that clean laundry eventually becomes
dirty and when it does, there is only one course of action ...
sort before you wash.

Janneth Mornan-Green

Closure

I covet a click:
a door swinging
to rest on its latch.
The subtle sound of closure.

III

I wish I were a bubble saving a computer screen;
I'd bounce but never break.

Emotions

My emotions wear an invisible cloak of silence
still as the brown pond where the ducks sit
patiently awaiting the reviving showers of April.

Janneth Mornan-Green

Tell Me ...

If you were here today
maybe the loaves and the fishes
would be small fry
and maybe you'd know that
seeing how you'd have to compete
with rappers on the street mouthing
lyrics with a modern beat.
You'd have to ride a riddim -
be a DJ playing the crowd like
a well tuned guitar
star; gazing at the other side
of a lake wouldn't be enough
and I wonder how you'd preach,
teach and do your tricks?
Would you do a talk show,
be a televangelist
or just chant down
Babylon in a crusade?
Would you have cable TV,
Internet and a blinking BB?
Tell me ...
if you were here,
how would you flex?

A Strength That Heals

My strength is neither a curse
nor an excuse for withholding your sympathy
it is not a plinth on which to rest
the burden of your belief
that strong women comfort, but don't cry
nurture but don't need

My strength sheaths feelings
conceals fury
salves the bruises of a broken heart

My strength perseveres,
stands firm on the shoulders of my belief
that while there is no prison as strong
as the one self-imposed,
there is no freedom greater than a strength that heals.

Janneth Mornan-Green

Zombie

I am led by half-dead people
who live by rote,
wrote the History that I study
to show myself approved;
proof that they lived
and that I
validate their lives.

Crossings

My skin says "I have lived"
crossed myriad boulevards
spoken to countless strangers.

I have seen many junctions like the one
I saw you hesitating to cross
and stretched a hand to point direction

the hand you took
to engrave on my palm the "otherness"
now etched deep into my lifeline

the otherness that makes me want to
erase the sameness
and forget that I too halt at crossings

restrained by neat stitches -
a trophy on my belly
like the wart that juts,
or the marks crisscrossing my womb
where you may hesitate to tread
once confronted with the evidence
that I have lived
and living came long before
you took your first breath.

Janneth Mornan-Green

Snapshot

The concrete steps are all that's left of the old house
just two where the front door used to be;
he stands at the top, his arms outstretched as if for flight
or in resignation at the house's plight.

Perhaps he's sifting his thoughts for a picture
the snapshot where plaid memories
relay simplicity in all its hues,
where barefoot jaunts overlap Sabbath services
or mischief, the anxieties of a young man's heart.

What secrets does your mind unearth I wonder;
suspicions of obeah, pain, a father's wrath, thoughts of murder?
Coloured marbles winking in the sunlight,
days dreaming, plotting escapades for the night?

Did you glimpse years of terror,
Bloody Mary scheming? Lord, the horror of
hurt, anger, love flipped to hate,
the fear of leaving.
Could you see your fate?

I look from this picture to your bier,
see you laying there,
arms stretched out
sleeping.

Morning Coffee

Platitudes come
like snow globes shaken,
confetti raining
copiously to settle
as sediments.
Long-stemmed promises
teem; pledges wrapped in rose petals
deftly packaged to conceal the prickles.
Words, like
repetitious polyps
populating the intestines of the unsuspecting,
morph into malignant memories
interred in the graveyard
of the mind.

Janneth Mornan-Green

Smoke, No Fire

Smoke clouded the evening
fanning fireless across the plains
to mingle with the mist that claims the flatlands at twilight.
The language of the landscape is transformed
into an obscure dialect
the myopic window cannot fathom
the message of the phantom spirals
or interpret the trajectory of the moon's persistent glide
over cowering trees, huddled beneath the malodorous blanket
awaiting the liberating breath of the east wind

the image teases your thoughts
but your dreams have
baked too long in the oven of the sun
the dew brings no relief,
no gentle breeze
to stir the ash of your imagination

here, in the mystery of your burning bush
no faceless voice promises emancipation

no ash-less thicket
offers a ticket to the miracle of freedom.

Knots

I have considered ending it;
un-knotting the cords
that fasten me to
the treadmill of hope.

I have given platitudes; paid penance,
but the gods of fidelity have not given back and
the red horse of rage is galloping
over the smooth places of my heart.

My bruises vibrate
with the rhythm of revenge,
and fractured flesh seeks ease
in the placid places of indifference.

Janneth Mornan-Green

Webmaster

Anancy awoke one morning and
decided to spin a web;
the details were so intricate
the construction immaculate
until she reached the centre
and dropped a stitch.
There began the unraveling …
now, like Humpty Dumpty
she's in a dilemma
'cause it's hell trying to hold that web together.

Sunday Stupor

Driving on Florida's I-95
with the day uncoiling like the highway
Aretha Franklin's
"Chain, chain, chain …
chain of fools"
intrudes, imposing a musical reminder.
The sky frowns,
its metal gray visage
pressed up close to the morning.
I watch the street signs pass,
a row of steely instructions
bringing me back to the reality
that the only certainty up ahead is the toll;
the toll, we all have to pay.

Janneth Mornan-Green

the edge (of the world)

hurt
like scalpel on bone severing
ligaments, tendons,
pain
a commandment, compelling feeling
teetering
on tear ducts like
the futility of ducks upon a dying pond

whirlpool
spinning faster than wheels
heated vortex of steel
burning, burning
consuming my mind,
torch searing my chest
my heart gasps
no breath

i'm falling
free falling, shattering
crystal pieces splintering
shards glistening
like lightening,
sheet lightening
blanketing, my emotions
writhing

i'm clutching
the fingers of the sun,
skin smouldering
falling,
i am falling
from the edge
of the world

On Hearing of Your Need for a Vessel

So, you're hoping for a vessel
to incubate, sprout your seeds?

Then, I guess any old receptacle will do.
A bucket, a cistern, a cup, a well
all should be the same to you.

Just baptise a shrew
in the holy water that you seem so reluctant
to spill, for fear that it will fall upon
ground that you may have to till.

Why nurture and mulch
or seek the grail washed with sacred dew
when all you need is … a vessel?

Janneth Mornan-Green

Guess Who?

Back then they burned heretics
I should have done the same
for they knew heretics are beyond redemption;
I hoped for conversion
so I doused the flames.
Now, guess who is at the stake;
burning?

When Memories Die

Like Daguerreotypes
lost in the modern maze of magical cameras and techno-jumble
I search for you among the faded images, concentrating hard to define your face,
the cute mole that used to perch just so against your chin
the way only you could laugh and wiggle your ear

I look for your imprint
your life's thread fastening the hem
of history
your legend fixed in
black and white.

But like ephemeral insects or flowers
your myth unravels

I glimpse your receding image and wonder;
Where do legends go when memories die?

Janneth Mornan-Green

Footnote

Difficult to accept
that I should become a footnote
or ellipses …
absent
from the words that made me tick
and the people who laughed at my jokes
or hated my progress

Difficult to grasp
my thoughts silenced;
a wrist-flick or curious bat of an eyelid
gathering dust on memory's shelf
or my stuff parted in lots,
the smell of my perfume
entombed in mothballs
as traces of me
dissolve into
the fading notes
of a forgettable
tune.

Land's End

And so, what's left?

The blue bird trimming its beak on the brittle bough?
The militant torch lily
that does not genuflect or bow its tonsured head
when the day breaks with 'woman' rain,
or audacious noon-heat bubbles the melting pitch?

She has known the discomfort of quietness
settling like fog over the nervous house,
crawling tiredly into frass-coated corners
mimicking marl that sleeps
in the ditch

she has tasted fear,
felt the furry fingers of desire
a peccant Eve caught in a fulgent glare,
paradise, a kernel sealed;
now glimpsed through an oxblood haze

she knows the June bug's orb
the leaf-covered spot
where the earth incubates its secret
and the brume-swept planes
from which the hills raise their bushy brows

to spy
stray images of Eden
dancing in a serein drift.
She has seen it all; now
what's left?

Janneth Mornan-Green

On Becoming My Legacy
(for Jean Asher)

We sit together
haloed in the tumult of our opinions
smoothing the seams the years have gathered,
our words press hard
rubbing against each other.

I ask you about life
you tell me about a river
rippling around a stone slowly sinking in its centre.
What is left is memory
deftly walking on water
side-stepping its reflection.

It's true enough
memory, laden store of
leaden sighs, grates on a moody morning
when the breeze rattles,
and 'woman tongue,' clapping
like worshippers in a pocomania frenzy,
call the ancestors to witness our folly.

Regrets queue,
anguished elephants
stroking dry bones, bleached testaments
of love lost , intimacies forgotten
and tears pool to flood the valleys
of a blurred landscape.

Could we have satisfied sufficiently
or surrendered unconditionally?
Can we like postcards in a box
or a key left under the mat
remain undisturbed
by the river's eddy?

Against the motion of the determined tide
sediments lie still beneath a stone.
There, the water does not run;
the legatee's songs are silent.

Janneth Mornan-Green

The Summer is Over

I hear the rebuttal of the quarrelsome wind
as it revives its dispute with the trees;
they would rather forget its contentions
its fervent breath sending
frissons through agitated leaves,
confounding the bickering, ant-eating birds
temporarily distracted from their gleaning.

Now the leaves have fallen
prey to the wind's seduction,
umber skinned, they lie
curled like frightened armadillos
while the birds resume their contending.

The summer is over
the leaves have fallen
and the shadows are long.

www.ingramcontent.com/pod-product-compliance
Lightning Source LLC
Chambersburg PA
CBHW032029040426
42448CB00006B/780